Living the Days of Lent 2008

Reflections on the Psalms

EDITED BY

Sister Anita M. Constance, SC

Paulist Press
New York / Mahwah, NJ

ISBN: 978-0-8091-4461-7

Published by Paulist Press
997 Macarthur Boulevard
Mahwah, New Jersey 07430

www.paulistpress.com

Printed and bound in the
United States of America

Introduction

The Book of Psalms...cries of joy, honesty, success, lamentation, and failure. Will we find ourselves among these sentiments and prayers? Most assuredly YES, because they are genuine expressions of the human spirit.

But what the psalmist has to teach us is twofold: his prayer came from the heart, and his heart was placed before God. The psalmist brought his needs, even his most basic needs, to God—turning to the saving, redeeming, forgiving, compassionate, gifting, and gentle God with his words and feelings.

As we make our Lenten journey this year, we might consider the ways of the psalmist and, without guilt or embarrassment, place the needs we discover in our self-reflection before our gracious God.

—Anita M. Constance, SC

Looking Within

*You desire truth in the inward being; therefore
teach me wisdom in my secret heart.*
Psalm 51:6

God lives, animates, and fills me day after day with the gifts of the Spirit—the wisdom of my secret heart. Now, during this Lenten season, God invites me to look within and see if something is still cluttering that sacred space. I've traveled this path before and will return here many times; but each time is equally essential to my growth in God and the quality of life that I will share with others.

This "looking within" will keep my eyes from straying to judgment about another's way of being and doing. This "looking within" will show me who God is and who I am *not*. This "looking within" will enable me to know God's mercy and forgiveness. This "looking within" will remind me to have mercy and to forgive. This "looking within" is the path and the grace of daily conversion.

**Today I will take some time to look within
and pray to find what God wishes to show me.**

Reflection:
Looking within, I find

_____

_____

Readings: Joel 2:12–18; Psalm 51; 2 Corinthians 5:20—6:2; Matthew 6:1–6, 16–18

Loved and Loving

*Their delight is in the law of the LORD, and on his
law they meditate day and night.*
Psalm 1:2

What a different person I would be, if I meditated on the Law of Love day and night! First to realize that I am loved...unconditionally loved by God. I find so many reasons to say, "I am not worthy." But truth is, worthiness is not an issue for God; it's *our* issue.

I believe that God does not want us to be stuck there. Always coming up against ourselves as we try to be good enough for God. I believe that our unworthiness is meant to free us—free us from a struggle that God never intended. God loves us just as we are, for no efforts of our own, on no merits of our own.

Is there another way to relate to God? Yes, I think we just *love. That's* the challenge. Love God and others as God has loved us. The Law of Love always moves us beyond ourselves. No longer preoccupied with worthiness, we can get on with living and loving...what God is all about. What Jesus showed us was most important.

**I will meditate on God's love for me and pass on
that love to someone I meet today.**

Reflection:
The energy of love leads me to

_____

_____

Readings: Deuteronomy 30:15–20; Psalm 1;
Luke 9:22–26

Broken and Blessed

The sacrifice acceptable to God is a broken spirit;
a broken and contrite heart, O God,
you will not despise.
Psalm 51:17

Jesus was held captive by the needs of others. He heard the cries of the poor; he touched and was touched. Jesus is the perfect reflection of his Father-God. He was and is the presence of our God who does not despise the weak, or crush the bruised reed.

A broken spirit and a contrite heart know the need for God. No one wants to be broken or sorrowful, but there is something about realizing that we are not self-sufficient; there is something about experiencing our imperfections that can make room for the divine in our lives.

Today the psalmist assures us that all will be well when we know our need for God. All will be well because God is with us, especially at those times. God desires to fill the cup of our lives in good times and in difficult ones.

Today I ask myself if I know my need for God.
I will name those places in my prayer.

Reflection:
My need for God

_____

_____

Readings: Isaiah 58:1–9; Psalm 51; Matthew 9:14–15

Truth and Life

Teach me your way, O LORD, that I may walk in your truth; give me an undivided heart to revere your name.
Psalm 86:11

To all seekers of truth: Suppose someone told you that TRUTH could be found in a cave on a distant mountain. That the journey there would be difficult and rigorous, possibly taking *years* to complete. Would you go? Would you be so dedicated as to make the sacrifices it would entail?

Yet God calls us to walk in the truth—to walk in the way and life of Jesus Christ. Living as disciples of Jesus is *not* easy. It means having an undivided heart, one focused on God alone. It is only this way, with our eyes on Jesus, that we can make the journey of our lives.

And when we arrive, we dare not just stand at truth's doorway and peek in. No, that would be absurd given the sacrifices that this journey entails. Lent invites us to take that final step inside and to see what truth really is—to discover that we are saved, forgiven, loved; that God celebrates our creation and has made us heirs of eternal life. Such truth requires a response. Let us pray for the courage to follow Jesus, who is the way to truth and life.

**How will I stay focused on Jesus today?
What will that mean to my life?**

Reflection:
God alone

_____

_____

Readings: Isaiah 58:9–14; Psalm 86; Luke 5:27–32

A Faithful Heart

Create in me a clean heart, O God,
and put a new and right spirit within me.
Psalm 51:10

Through the ups and downs and the ins and outs of life's journey, our time with God and the quality of that core relationship may ebb and flow. In the joys of life, do we turn to God the creator of all good things in grateful praise? And in the trying times of life, do we keep our eyes fixed on the God who has always held us and never abandoned us?

The psalmist prays for a steadfast spirit—one that remains faithful to God through the sorrows and trials as well as the joyful celebrations. May our prayer be the same.

Wherever I am today—on a mountaintop or valley or plain—I will turn to God in trust and ask God to renew a steadfast spirit within me.

Reflection:
My need to trust

_____

_____

_____

Readings: Genesis 2:7–9; 3:1–7; Psalm 51;
Romans 5:12–19; Matthew 4:1–11

Self-Reflection

Let the words of my mouth and the [thought] of my heart be acceptable to you.
Psalm 19:14

The psalmist today invites us to listen to the words of our mouths and to reflect on the thoughts of our hearts. We speak and write many words each day, and our thoughts, both fleeting and enduring, are myriad. Sometimes words may pour out of our mouths (or computers) without much prior thought. Likewise, some of our actions may result more from impulse than from reflection. We are challenged today to ground our words and our thoughts in our hearts, united with the heart of Jesus. They will then find favor before God.

Today I will pause for a moment before I speak, before I hit "send" and before I act, remembering first the God who dwells within me and within the other.

Reflection:
Thinking with the heart

_____

_____

_____

Readings: Leviticus 19:1–2, 11–18; Psalm 19; Matthew 25:31–46

God, Our Refuge

*The LORD is near to the brokenhearted,
and saves the crushed in spirit.*
Psalm 34:18

There certainly are times in our lives when we are full of fear or distress, times when we are brokenhearted or crushed. While our faith tells us that we will never be destroyed by all the trouble that seems to surround us, despair may lead us to question this. We are not the creators of our lives and neither are we the saviors. Our lives are not solely our own; they belong to God. It is in times of fear and distress, sorrow and hardship, that God urges us to look beyond ourselves. God's love is deliverance from all that we fear and all that distresses us. God will save us from destruction and console us in our sorrow, if we but open our hearts to the life of grace within.

**Today I will turn to God with a difficulty of life,
realizing it is not a burden I have to carry alone,
but one that God will share with me. I will also
listen to another if the opportunity presents itself
and share in his or her burden or pain.**

Reflection:
The burdens I give to God are

_____

_____

_____

Readings: Isaiah 55:10–11; Psalm 34; Matthew 6:7–15

Merciful God

*According to your abundant mercy
blot out my transgressions.*
Psalm 51:1

Our sense of justice may be compared at times to a balance: I will forgive you *if* you forgive me. God's justice, however, reaches far beyond *our* measuring, and God's compassion is without bounds. We, too, are called to move out of our comfortable reciprocity to love and to forgive others with boundless charity. When we broaden our sense of justice, we experience a glimpse of the greatness of God's compassion toward us.

Today I will call to mind someone who has recently hurt or offended me, and I will ask God to help me to be compassionate toward him or her.

Reflection:
I desire to forgive

_____

_____

_____

Readings: Jonah 3:1–10; Psalm 51; Luke 11:29–32

Unconditional Love

The LORD will fulfill his purpose for me.
Psalm 138:8

God is with us on all the days of our journey and asks us to be faithful in our companionship and discipleship. There are many stops and starts, it seems, and some may even appear to be regressive. God began the good work in us at the time of our baptism and God will continue it throughout our lives. We may start and stop, but God will continue with us faithfully, completing much good within and through us. May we be open to his actions today and always.

I will be attentive to God's action in my life today, calling me to love, perform a good work, or merely be present to another in need.

Reflection:
The call to discipleship leads me to

_____

_____

_____

Readings: Esther C: 12, 14–16, 23–25; Psalm 138; Matthew 7:7–12

Friday, *February 15*

Trusting Silence

*LORD, hear my voice! Let your ears be attentive
to the voice of my supplications!*
Psalm 130:2

Does God really hear our prayers, or are we merely speaking to ourselves? Sometimes we may wonder if God hears us, for nothing seems to "happen" when we pray. It may seem as if we are speaking to ourselves or calling into the great abyss only to hear our own voice resound in the emptiness. And so, with the psalmist, we cry out for God's attention. We pray that this time we will know and hear God's voice in response, filling the emptiness and calming our fears.

Today I will listen attentively to someone who comes to me in need, and I will bring that person's needs as well as mine to God in confidence and trust.

Reflection:
Lord, hear my prayer

Readings: Ezekiel 18:21–28; Psalm 130;
Matthew 5:20–26

Saturday, *February 16*

The Unexpected

Happy are those...who seek him
with their whole heart.
Psalm 119:2

Where do we seek God? Do we look in all the ordinary places: churches and nature, and people we love? Do we search, too, in hidden and out-of-the-ordinary places? In the weeds and in the thorns; in the corners and in the shadows? Sometimes from unexpected places and people we hear God's voice most clearly. Listen to the person near you in line at the supermarket. Listen to the one who cleans the office. Listen to the one who seems an annoyance. Listen to the one who begs at your door.

I will seek you today, Lord, in a place where I do not usually look. I will listen to your voice from someone to whom my ear is unaccustomed to hearing.

Reflection:
Seeking God

_____

_____

_____

Readings: Deuteronomy 26:16–19; Psalm 119; Matthew 5:43–48

In the Gaze of God

Truly the eye of the LORD is on those who fear him,
on those who hope in God's steadfast love.
Psalm 33:18

Ojo de Dios, or Eye of God, is a folk art form originating with the Huichol Indians of northern Mexico and the Aymara Indians of Bolivia. *Ojo de Dios* is a sacred symbol representing God's presence, power, and care. The brightly colored yarn, tightly woven through concentric rows into a diamond pattern, is simple in form but riveting. It centers attention, holds the connection, and reminds the believer of the penetrating, all-encompassing, and sheltering presence of God's spirit—in the universe that contains and supports us, in the give-and-take of relationships, in the creative process in which we participate, in the pull of our longings. The compassionate Eye of God rests on all who hope in God.

As I begin this second week of my Lenten journey,
I will make time to rest in the loving gaze of God.

Reflection:
Realizing God's presence

_____

_____

_____

Readings: Genesis 12:1–4; Psalm 33;
2 Timothy 1:8–10; Matthew 17:1–9

Generations of Faith

*Do not remember against us the iniquities of our
ancestors...and forgive us our sins for your
name's sake...from generation to generation
we will recount your praise.*
Psalm 79: 8–9, 13

In this communal lament, the psalmist begs God to hear
the people's prayers for forgiveness and protection, and
then boldly asserts that God's own promise, God's
integrity, is at stake in this plea. Age upon age God has
promised to be with the Israelites. We, too, journey to God
with others and draw from this communal treasure. Our
forebears in faith, generation upon generation, traveled
this path before us in an unbroken thread, holding fast to
God's promise.

Previous generations have shaped us—our world-
view, genetic predispositions, patterns of behavior, abili-
ties, and limitations, even the framework of our faith. This
inheritance is a mixture of glory and shadow, which we
carry for awhile and then gift to those who will follow.

**Today I will reflect on the particular expression of faith
that has formed me, winnowing out what I find most
precious, praising God for the life that is mine.**

Reflection:
The gift of others

_____

_____

Readings: Daniel 9:4–10; Psalm 79; Luke 6:36–38

Thanksgiving Enfleshed

*Those who bring thanksgiving as their sacrifice
honor me; to those who go the right way
I will show the salvation of God.*
Psalm 50:23

These lines from Psalm 50 are believed to be the conclusion of an ancient covenant-renewal liturgy. God, the righteous judge, had rebuked the Israelites for their grievous wrongdoing. Many of their religious rituals with their prescribed sacrificial offerings were unacceptable to God because they were empty actions. Sacrifice offered without the interior dispositions of humility and thanksgiving, and the intention of walking in God's way, is meaningless. Likewise the traditional Lenten practices of prayer, fasting, and almsgiving *alone* do not deepen our relationship with God. Conversion of mind and heart, awakening us to the presence and action of God in our world, is salvific.

**With Meister Eckhart, the fourteenth-century German
mystic, I ask God, who has given me so much,
for one additional gift—a grateful heart.**

Reflection:
Conversion calls me

_____

_____

Readings: Isaiah 1:10, 16–20; Psalm 50;
Matthew 23:1–12

Resting in God

*Into your hand I commit my spirit;...I trust in you,
O LORD; I say "You are my God."
My times are in your hand.*
Psalm 31:5, 14–15

People of ancient Near Eastern cultures believed that major events of life, such as birth and death, were fixed or determined by the gods. The Israelites' understanding of their covenant relationship with Yahweh was influenced by this underlying societal belief. Here the psalmist expresses a serene confidence and trust in God, secure in believing that God who is good desires only good for all. The very human image of God's "hand" holding our times, our lives, our whole world, evokes many dimensions of meaningful relationship: safekeeping, power, protection, pledge or promise, commitment, support, and companionship, to name a few.

Which dimensions of God's care speak most strongly to me today?

**Today I will consider my own hands, reflect on their
innate beauty and power, and remember
the many ways my hands express
God's care for others.**

Reflection:
I am held by God

_____

_____

Readings: Jeremiah 18:18–20; Psalm 31;
Matthew 20:17–28

Water and the Spirit

Happy are those...[who] are like trees planted by streams of water, which yield their fruit in its season.
Psalm 1:1, 3

For trees—as for all living things—water is elemental, absolutely essential. Without water there is no life, no fruit. "It comes down in one form but works in many forms…. [Water] becomes white in the lily, red in the rose, purple in violets and hyacinths…" (Cyril of Jerusalem).

The roots of the trees sink deep into the banks of streams, drawing nutrients from the earth through the moisture, and in turn, the leaves of the trees replenish the earth and the roots strengthen and stabilize the banks. It is a magnificent, intricate, interdependent community of life. We are invited into contemplation of this one mutually interconnected world to receive its truth.

We, together with the whole community of creation, are the trees; and the water, the sustainer of life, is the Spirit. Like water, the Spirit is refreshing, nourishing, creative, harmonizing. How do I understand my place in this interdependent community of life? Where do I perceive traces of water and the vivifying Spirit in my world?

Today I will handle water reverently.

Reflection:
Community with creation

Readings: Jeremiah 17:5–10; Psalm 1; Luke 16:19–31

Friday, *February 22*

Abundant Love

You prepare a table before me in the presence
of my enemies, you anoint my head with oil;
my cup overflows.
Psalm 23:5

Psalm 23 exudes confidence and trust. The psalmist depicts God as both shepherd and host, images conveying to the Israelites good leadership and providence. A shepherd guided sheep to safety, and a host fulfilled the sacred obligation of welcoming and providing for guests. In a nomadic culture, hospitality to friend and stranger could be the difference between life and death.

The psalmist revels in God's providential care imaged in the banquet table and in the gracious gestures of hospitality, even in the face of danger or hostility. In the anointing, we understanding refreshment for the traveler, and in the overflowing cup, we sense abundance. God's bounty and largesse—beyond our ability to imagine—is lavished on us and on all humanity. What are the gifts which I long to have spread before me?

When have I experienced hospitality? How will I offer hospitality to those I encounter today?

Reflection:
The providence of God

_____

_____

Readings: 1 Peter 5:1–4; Psalm 23; Matthew 16:13–19

Healing God

Bless the LORD, O my soul, and do not forget all his benefits—who forgives all your iniquities, who heals all your diseases.
Psalm 103:2–3

In both the Hebrew and Christian scriptures, illness and disease were associated with sin. Jesus' healing actions in the gospels bring physical healing, but always point to deeper realities—lack of faith, rifts in the community, intentional blindness. All of us stand in need of healing in one form or another—perhaps from physical disease, accidents, or the limitations of aging, or perhaps from shattered relationships, painful memories, loss, trauma, or depression. The portal to healing always takes us to the realm of the Spirit. It is said that we dress wounds, but God alone heals. Cures are attested to by empirical evidence and scientific data, but healing is an internal process by which one is made whole or restored to well-being. What in my life needs healing? What in our world cries out for healing?

How am I called to heal this day?

Reflection:
The healings within me

_____

_____

Readings: Micah 7:14–15, 18–20; Psalm 103;
Luke 15:1–3, 11–32

Giving Thanks

Let us come into his presence with thanksgiving.
Psalm 95:2

God, giver of all life and goodness, thank you for this time right now to be still, to let go, and to be present to you in gratitude. For a few moments I want to say "Thank You" instead of "Please...."

THANK YOU
>for my parents, life, family, and friends.
>for inviting me to follow you.
>for the love I have received and have been able to give.
>for the ability to see, speak, walk, and choose.
>for dreams, desires, and hopes.
>for the varied circumstances and events along my journey.
>for the beauty of creation—sky, sea, the earth.
>for the sacredness and uniqueness of all living beings.

THANK YOU
>for the share in the cross and resurrection of your Son.
>for the surprises of your Spirit.

THANK YOU, my God, for you!

What shall I do today to put flesh on my thanksgiving?

Reflection:
I am most thankful for

_____

_____

Readings: Exodus 17:3–7; Psalm 95;
Romans 5:1–2, 5–8; John 4:5–42

Longings

My soul thirsts for God, for the living God.
Psalm 42:2

We experience moments, days, months, and even years of fear, anxiety, and waiting. During these times, O God, we bombard you with questions: Why? Why *now*? Why *me*? How much longer? Will I make it? Where are you? Have you forgotten me?

We feel parched, dry, lifeless. We long for your touch, your healing, for You—the Living God,—who alone can quench our thirst and satisfy our longing.

Then there are those fleeting moments when a longing for you swells within our hearts in quiet, stillness, or solitude, through your unexpected surprises, at the sight of the beauty of a sunset, the majesty of a mountain, a glimpse of love.

We long for you, O God, our strength, our joy, our all.

**In stillness and quiet I will take some time
to rest in the arms of God.**

Reflection:
My soul thirsts

_____

_____

_____

Readings: 2 Kings 5:1–15; Psalms 42, 43; Luke 4:24–30

Struggling with God

Make me to know your ways, O LORD;
teach me your paths.
Psalm 25:4

How different our ways are from your ways, O God!

We put each other to the test—the test of color, nationality, age, and religious beliefs.
We judge, ignore, criticize, and expect recompense and recognition.
We choose the path of ease, selfishness, and convenience.
We forget how to sacrifice, share, and collaborate.
We prefer to control and dictate both individually and collectively.
We let fear, guilt, and pride paralyze us and keep us from knowing your love, O God.

Your paths, O God, are those of steadfast love and faithfulness. You are merciful, compassionate, forgiving, and all-embracing. May your Spirit lead and guide us in all your ways!

May just one thought, word, or deed of mine today be one of compassion or forgiveness, affirmation, or trust.

Reflection:
The ways of compassion

_____

_____

Readings: Daniel 3:25, 34–43; Psalm 25;
Matthew 18:21–35

Blessings

[God] sends out his command to the earth;
[God's] word runs swiftly.
Psalm 147:15

How wonderful your works, O God! How bountiful your care!

At your command the birds of the air, the fish in the sea, and all animals are nourished. At your word the heavens provide clouds to bring down rain and snow to water the earth.

You delight in all of creation, especially in loving each one of us. You call us by name. You shower your blessings upon us. You bring us peace. You heal the brokenhearted and lift up the downtrodden. You nourish us with the finest of wheat.

It pleases you when we reach out to others, and when we trust in your steadfast love. You rejoice and are delighted with us when we are fully alive in your love. How right it is to sing praises to you, my God!

I will begin and end this day in gratitude and attentiveness to God's word spoken in all of creation, most especially within the depths of my heart.

Reflection:
God's word alive in me

_____

_____

Readings: Deuteronomy 4:1, 5–9; Psalm 147; Matthew 5:17–19

Hearts of Flesh

*O that today you would listen to his voice!
Do not harden your hearts.*
Psalm 95:7b–8a

We hear, but do we listen? Our eyes and ears are bombarded and saturated with words, noise, radio, TV, newspapers. All vie for our time and attention.

But do we listen to your communication of yourself to us, O God? Are we aware of the new ideas, the desires and dreams you put into our hearts, the strength you place into our wills, the calming of our emotions, the whispers of your love?

At times we are distracted from listening to what is expressed behind or beyond the spoken word. Is it the pain of a hurting friend, the cry of a child ignored or abandoned by a parent, the silent pleading for companionship by an elderly parent or neighbor?

Transform our hardened hearts, O God, to softened, listening hearts—hearts sensitive, receptive, and responsive to you, life, and love.

**I will express this gift of a listening heart
wherever God leads me this day.**

Reflection:
Where I need softening

_____

_____

Readings: Jeremiah 7:23–28; Psalm 95; Luke 11:14–23

Compassionate God

I am the LORD your God.
Psalm 81:10

Creator God, you call us to life and love. *You* are Love. Yet we doubt and even turn our backs on Love—love of you, self, and others. We fail to heed your voice spoken in ages past and in our own time. We create our own gods—glamour, riches, ambition, security, and momentary pleasures become powerful and persuasive. We take control from you and choose our own way.

Still, faithfully, you rescue us over and over. You desire our hearts. You hear our plea for mercy; you shoulder our burden; you feed us with the finest of wheat and honey (v. 16)—inviting us to let go and fall into your embrace of new life.

Let us live today in gratitude for our merciful God by being merciful to another.

Reflection:
God's mercy toward me

_____

_____

_____

Readings: Hosea 14:2–10; Psalm 81; Mark 12:28–34

An Honest Heart

Have mercy on me, O God,
according to your steadfast love.
Psalm 51:1

In his autobiography, *The Seven Storey Mountain,* following a soul-searching experience, Thomas Merton wrote, "I was overwhelmed with a sudden and profound insight into the misery and corruption of my soul....I really began to pray—out of the very roots of my life and of my being...."

Loving God, we come before you as we are—in our goodness, but also with our baggage, struggles, failures, and sin.

Create in us a clean heart, O God, and put a new and right spirit within us. Restore to us the joy of your salvation and sustain in us a willing spirit (vs. 10–12).

In our examination of conscience tonight,
let us ask for the grace to see ourselves honestly
and lovingly, as God sees us.

Reflection:
I am forgiven

_____

_____

_____

Readings: Hosea 6:1–6; Psalm 51; Luke 18:9–14

Shepherd of My Heart

The LORD is my shepherd; there is nothing I lack....
I fear no evil; for you are with me; your rod
and your staff—they comfort me.
Psalm 23:1, 4

As a shepherd keeps watch over his sheep you care for
    me, Lord.
All things come from your hand;
You supply all that is necessary for my good.
You nourish and nurture me with your care.
I am always in your sight.
Before a word is spoken, you attend to my needs.
What more could I ask? You are the desire of my heart.
How foolish I am to seek after what is of no avail;
What gives no measure to my life.
You, Lord, are sufficient; with you I possess all.
You carry me when I am weak, and give me your strength
    when I am frightened.
Take my hand and bring me into your banquet of love.
Give me the grace that brings eternal life.

Today I commit myself to allow my
Shepherd to take the lead.

Reflection:
God comforts me

_____

_____

Readings: 1 Samuel 16:1, 6–7; Psalm 23;
Ephesians 5:8–14; John 9:1–41

Saving God

*O LORD my God, I cried to you for help,
and you have healed me.*
Psalm 30:2

How compassionate and caring you are, Lord!
I need not fear for you are at my side.
You protect me and give yourself to me.
You deliver me from all that will harm me.
You give me your blessing and take me by the hand.
You hear my cries and wipe my tears from my face.

Help me to hear the cries around me.
Help me to step outside myself and
   to give to those who look to me for help.

I will be a healing presence to another, this day.

Reflection:
The Lord has heard my cries

_____

_____

_____

Readings: Isaiah 65:17–21; Psalm 30; John 4:23–54

God, My Deliverer

The LORD of hosts is with us;
the God of Jacob is our refuge.
Psalm 46:7

I tremble and give in to my fear.
I look around me and there is turmoil and despair.
I call to you, Lord, hear the words
   that come from the depths of my being.
With you I can do all things;
   without you I can do nothing, and all seems useless.
Show yourself, Lord, let me see the radiance of your
   right hand and arm.
If I stumble and fall, you lift me up and take from
   me all fear.
Give me your protection for you are
   truly my stronghold and my deliverer.
You are the God of my ancestors,
   the God who hears my cry.

I will take time today and name the ways
God has delivered me.

Reflection:
God upholds my life

_____

_____

Readings: Ezekiel 47:1–9, 12; Psalm 46;
John 5:1–3, 5–16

Wednesday, *March 5*

Merciful Love

*The LORD is gracious and merciful, slow to anger
and abounding in steadfast love.
The LORD is good to all, and his compassion
is over all that he has made.*
Psalm 145:8–9

Lord, you have been merciful and compassionate to me so many times. Yet I hold back my mercy and compassion from my friend, my neighbor, my coworker, those I live with. I seek mercy but my anger gets in the way. And I turn from others, refusing them my compassion.

Many times my willingness to extend mercy has to do with who it is that asks for my forgiveness, and yet, Lord, your love and mercy are given to all your people...unconditionally. I need your help, Lord, that I might be more ready to love your children—my sisters and brothers. Give me a merciful and forgiving heart; let compassion dwell within me.

**I will be mindful of God's call to compassion
as I interact with others throughout the day.**

Reflection:
My unconditional love

_____

_____

Readings: Isaiah 49:8–15; Psalm 145; John 5:17–30

Thursday, *March 6*

Held by God

They made a calf at Horeb and worshipped a cast image. They exchanged the glory of God for the image of an ox that eats grass.
Psalm 106:19–20

How many calves and bulls have I worshipped, Lord? Power, prestige, money, the finest clothes, the first places? I, too, have worshiped false gods and find myself following after the latest fads. I want so much to belong, and yet the truth before me is hidden from my eyes.

You tell me I am yours. You have called me by name. You know the number of hairs on my head. You hold me in the palm of your hand. All life comes from you and blessings in abundance. You care for me. You give me your love and call me Beloved! Forgive me, Lord; may I follow only your path and walk after you alone.

Today, with all my being, I will worship the God who dwells within me.

Reflection:
Caring for God within me

_____

_____

_____

Readings: Exodus 32:7–14; Psalm 106; John 5:31–47

Lost and Found

The LORD is near to the brokenhearted,
and saves the crushed in spirit. Many are the
afflictions of the righteous, but the LORD
rescues them from them all.
Psalm 34:18–19

There are times, Lord, when I am bowed down under
   my load.
Trials and heartache follow wherever I go.
The weight of my sorrow overpowers me
   and I am crushed beneath it.
My life seems like one lost and not able to go on,
   yet in due time I know you will hear and answer me.
You have always been my refuge in each season of my life.
I have come to you and you turned your face toward me.
You hear me calling out to you.
Be present to me and give me your blessing,
   deliver me from all my fears that I might sing
   your praise.

**I ask for the gift of trust that I might rely
on God, all my life.**

Reflection:
My fears

_____

_____

Readings: Wisdom 2:1, 12–22; Psalm 34;
John 7:1–2, 10, 25–30

Just Believer

*...judge me, O LORD, according to my righteousness
and according to the integrity that is in me.
O let the evil of the wicked come to an end,
but establish the righteous, you who test the minds
and hearts, O righteous God.*
Psalm 7:9–10

I ask for justice, Lord, and yet I know that I
     cannot claim to be completely blameless before you.
It is you who have taken my guilt from me.
You have wiped the slate of my life clean.
Yet suffering and malice are all around me,
     creating unbearable hardships for your children—
     persecuting those who seek to walk your path,
     bringing endless destruction to the innocent.
I call to you, hear me, O Lord.
Come with the might of your justice and mercy,
     for you are faithful and fill with goodness those
     who seek you.

**Who are the innocent victims in my world today?
I will do something to lift them up.**

Reflection:
When my heart is tested I

_____

_____

Readings: Jeremiah 11:18–20; Psalm 7; John 7:40–53

Waiting with Trust

With Holy Week on the horizon, we move further into our Lenten reflections. Psalm 130 and its repeated refrain take on profound meaning. Who of us cannot cry out with the psalmist: "Out of the depths," of my spiritual, physical, psychic frailty, "I cry to you, O LORD. LORD, hear my voice! Let your ears be attentive to the voice of my supplications!" (vv. 1–2).

Who among us is deaf and blind to the opportunities wasted as we have tried to grow as disciples of the Lord Jesus? Who has not experienced the wounds we inflict on ourselves and others, when we allow sin and selfishness to find a home within us? But instead of giving into despair, we can trust as did the psalmist and pray, "I wait for the LORD, my soul waits, and in his word I hope" (v. 5). We can pray this with confidence because "with the LORD there is steadfast love, and with him is great power to redeem"(v. 7).

**Today I will lay, before Jesus, a fear or feeling
of hopelessness. I will place it in his hands
and trust in his healing.**

Reflection:
I will trust God to

_____

_____

_____

Readings: Ezekiel 37:12–14; Psalm 130;
Romans 8:8–11; John 11:1–45

Shepherd Me

Psalm 23 is probably one of the most often-prayed psalms by Christians and Jews. Its theme of confidence in God's provident care is timeless. All of us have experienced the joys and sorrows of life. I think of Saint Elizabeth Ann Seton, whose life was filled with great joys as a wife, mother, friend, convert to Catholicism, and founder of a religious community. This psalm was her favorite.

"The Lord is my shepherd, I shall not want" (v. 1). Elizabeth knew this in her bones. "Even though I walk through the darkest valley, I fear no evil; for you are with me…" (v. 5). Separation and death of loved ones were continuing experience throughout her life, as was misunderstanding and rejection when she converted to the Catholic faith.

Yet, especially after founding the Sisters of Charity, she could pray: "Surely goodness and mercy shall follow me all the days of my life, and I shall dwell in the house of the Lord my whole life long" (v. 6).

I will pray Psalm 23, and choose a particular verse to carry with me throughout this day.

Reflection:
God shepherds me

_____

_____

_____

Readings: Daniel 13:1–9, 15–17, 19–30;
Psalm 23; John 8:1–11

God of My Heart

Hear my prayer, O LORD; let my cry come to you.
Psalm 102:1

The readings for today stress God's mercy and forgiveness. God will be OUR GOD even when our faith is weak, and our awareness of our weakness and sin can be ignored no longer. It is then that we can only pray, "Do not hide your face from me in the day of my distress. Incline your ear to me; answer me speedily in the day when I call" (v. 4).

In this time in history, many evils within and around us seem to be overwhelming. It is just at a time like this that we must turn with confidence to our God and believe with the psalmist: [The Lord] "looked down from his holy height, from heaven the LORD looked at the earth, to hear the groans of the prisoners, to set free those who were doomed to die" (vv. 19–20). Yes, we know in our hearts that our God will be our help and support.

**I will recall God's compassion for me today
and make this a prayer of thanksgiving.**

Reflection:
My prayer for courage

_____

_____

_____

Readings: Numbers 21:4–9; Psalm 102; John 8:21–30

Blessed Be God

Daniel tells the story of the three young men who chose faithfulness to God over threat of torture and death. The God of both Jews and Christians is Creator of the universe, the final Source of all that is. Acknowledging that reality, we lift our hands and pray, "Blessed are you, O Lᴏʀᴅ, God..." (Dan 3:52).

In a kind of chant, we give voice to our faith: "Blessed are you, O Lᴏʀᴅ, the God of our ancestors..."(v. 52). Naming elements of God's universal power, we sing: "Blessed are you in the temple of your holy glory....Blessed are you who look into the depths from your throne upon the cherubim..." (vv. 53–54).

The three young men sang this prayer in the face of probable death. As disciples of Jesus, we are also invited to pray in times of danger, sickness, failure, temptation, or doubt. It is a prayer often made with our eyes squeezed shut and our hearts open wide to the power of God in our lives.

**How shall I pray, this day, when I am faced
with my vulnerability?**

Reflection:
Faith carries me

_____

_____

_____

Readings: Daniel 3:14–20, 52–56, 91–92, 95;
John 8:31–42

Lenten Thoughts

[The LORD] is mindful of his covenant forever.
Psalm 105:8

Faithfulness to the covenant is an important theme for meditation during Lent. Often we forget that through our baptism we have become covenanted with God and the Christian community. Through grace we are enabled to be faithful to that covenant. "Seek the LORD and his strength; seek his presence continually. Remember the wonderful works he has done, his miracles, and the judgments he uttered..." (vv. 4–5). Responding to the infinite graciousness of our God is a lifetime effort and grace. The effort lies in our degree of commitment; the grace is gift. But God is gracious and good; we can rely on his faithfulness.

**Today I will focus on some of the aspects
of my personal covenant with God and others.**

Reflection:
Remembering God

_____

_____

_____

Readings: Genesis 17:3–9; Psalm 105; John 8:51–59

Following Jesus

The scripture readings for today recount the struggles of the prophet Jeremiah and of Jesus. Both were preaching a very *unpopular* message that would force their listeners to respond to God's call to reform. Their experience could have echoed the psalmist, "In my distress I called upon the LORD....From his temple he heard my voice..." (Ps 18:6). In faith and trust, they would pray: "I love you, O LORD, my strength. The LORD is my rock, my fortress, my deliverer..." (vv. 1–2).

As followers of Jesus, we know how hard it is to be consistently faithful. We too have heard the call to repent and to follow Jesus with greater fidelity. Yet, it is often easier to listen to the ways of our culture and to reject a call to faithfulness. Sometimes, we too might want to cry out: "The cords of death encompassed me; torrents of perdition assailed me..." (v. 4).

Lent is about repairing and deepening our faithfulness to God. We must be willing to lay our truth before God, and struggle for fidelity to the way, truth, and life of Jesus...especially when such choices are unpopular.

I will spend some time in prayer today reflecting on ways I am called to be faithful.

Reflection:
Choosing truth, seeking justice

_____

_____

Readings: Jeremiah 20:10–13; Psalm 18; John 10:31–42

Savior

Once again, God is seen as a shepherd who always cares for his flock. On the brink of Holy Week, the most sacred period of our Lenten journey, we walk these last days with joy and trust in a God who never abandons us: "Hear the word of the LORD, O nations, and declare it in the coastlands far away; say, 'He who scattered Israel will gather him, and will keep him as a shepherd a flock'" (Jer 31:10).

It is a time of greater commitment to God and neighbor, making the reign of God more present in our world. With the psalmist, we pray: The LORD has ransomed Jacob, and has redeemed him from hands too strong for him" (v. 11). We can pray this with confidence because we know that this is the Lord's work more than ours.

Redemption is at hand! We have been redeemed, but we must also experience that abundant life in new ways each day. Lent gives us this opportunity.

**Today I will ponder the very real ways
I have been redeemed.**

Reflection:
Redeeming grace in my life

_____

_____

_____

Readings: Ezekiel 37:21–28; Jeremiah 31:10–13; John 11:45–57

Our Jerusalem

Today I recall the words of a popular hymn: "I have set my heart on the way; the journey is my destiny" ("Jerusalem, My Destiny"). The *journey* of life *is* our *destiny;* so it was for Jesus. And, like Jesus, we cannot turn away from this path because it is only in living each day well that we become his disciples.

We know where the journey led Jesus—to the cross. It will lead us there as well. It has led some of us there already. It is the deaths of "everyday" that lead to resurrection. But, like Jesus, we must die willingly. That is not easy to do; certainly God knows.

Jesus did not *want* to die; he struggled with that in the Garden of Olives. But the sweating of blood and his cries to God did not take away from his final "yes." And because of this, we can identify with him all the more. All the struggling we may do, each time we are up against a wall or plunged into the world of loss and grief, does not take away from our final "yes"...our final "thy will be done."

Today I will reflect on the story of Jerusalem and the journey I share with Jesus. I will prepare myself for the holiest of weeks to come.

Reflection:
Your will be done

_____

_____

Readings: *Procession:* Matthew 21:1–11; *Mass:* Isaiah 50:4–7; Psalm 22; Philippians 2:6–11; Matthew 26:14—27:66

Holy Desires

Wait for the LORD; *be strong.*
Psalm 27:14

An Irish blessing goes, "May you be in heaven half an hour before the devil knows you are dead." Apt petition for one whose impatience and weakness stand out in bold relief against the backdrop of Holy Week. Yes, I have been stripped again this Lent of the façade of self-sufficiency. I am utterly dependent on your mercy, Lord, now, and at the hour of my death. Look under my impatience and see the desire that fuels it. Strengthen your grace in me, forged in the fire of desire.

Today, Lord, I will notice when I strive to run ahead of your grace, when I seek to be strong apart from you. I will let each moment of waiting—at an elevator or traffic light, for the slow steps of a small child or aged parent—be a concrete reminder that I wait for, I long for you. And I wait not just for heaven.... "I believe that I shall see the goodness of the LORD in the land of the living." Psalm 27:13

Reflection:
I wait for

_____

_____

Readings: Isaiah 42:1–7; Psalm 27; John 12:1–11

Words of Truth

...incline your ear to me and save me.
Psalm 71:2

Not enough, my God, to ask that you hear me, or even that you listen, but I implore you to cock your head and cup your ear so as not to miss a word of what I have to say. Still, I must ask: Have all my words been such that I welcome your rapt attention to each one?

Lord, today, "my mouth will tell of your righteous acts, of your deeds of salvation all day long" (Psalm 71:15). And I will incline my ear to someone whose voice has not been heard or to whom I have not listened well lately.

Reflection:
Listening to God

_____

_____

_____

Readings: Isaiah 49:1–6; Psalm 71;
John 13:21–33, 36–38

Fire of Love

It is zeal for your house that has consumed me.
Psalm 69:9

What projects, peeves, penchants, or plans have consumed *me* thus far in this holiest of weeks?

Lord Jesus, you lived your life with such desire for the will of God that you were consumed by it in the span of a short human life. Give me the grace to live with your commitment and focus.

Today, I will clean out my larder of desires to create a space so wide and deep that zeal for your house, your people, YOU will consume me this Easter Triduum.

Reflection:
Consumed by love when

_____

_____

_____

Readings: Isaiah 50:4–9; Psalm 69; Matthew 26:14–25

Acceptance

O LORD, I am your servant; I am your servant....
You have loosed my bonds.
Psalm 116:16

Jesus, free, broke bread, even with the doubter, the denier, and the betrayer. Jesus, free, placed his trust in Peter to lead the church; Peter, who, missing the meaning, protested when Jesus removed his robe, took the lowest place, and washed his feet. Jesus, free, at the appointed time, entrusted "do this in memory of me" to his fragile, fallible friends.

You've stooped low, freeing Jesus, to loose my bonds. Yet how easily I slip back into them, pull them tight, and feel the victim, not the liberated one you have made me. I choose to learn from Peter and submit to your healing touch, despite my protests that I know best what in myself and others most needs a good scrubbing.

With each step I take today I will remember how good it is to follow you on feet that are both free and clean. I will walk in the direction that leads me closer to you.

Reflection:
Jesus, set me free

_____

_____

Readings: Exodus 12:1–8, 11–14; Psalm 116;
1 Corinthians 11:23–26; John 13:1–15

Gift of Time

sinless Servant, spurned, smitten...
deepest darkness descends
Death
nights the noontime

My times are in your hand. Psalm 31:15

...yet, this time, too, also in your hand:
only One offered
faithful fulfillment finished
Light from Light
Labors in love
through the darkness
for Eternal time

My times, in your hand, have not been cast off, nor have they slipped through your fingers. Do I live each moment, day, and year of them mindful that these "times" are yours, and I am living the gift of them in each choice I make? Am I graceful and accepting when your hand carries "my" time someplace other than my choosing?

**Today, Lord, each time I must endure some type
of suffering, be it a simple annoyance or a deep hurt,
help me to recall that this time, too, is in
your hand...and you guide me.**

Reflection:
The Hand of God upon me

_____

_____

Readings: Isaiah 52:13—53:12; Psalm 31;
Hebrews 4:14–16; 5:7–9; John 18:1—19:42

Holy Saturday, *March 22*

Waiting for Dawn

*Weeping may linger for the night,
but joy comes with the morning.*
Psalm 30:5

The night is spent at dusk on this holiest of nights; morning dawns with the new paschal fire. The Good News cannot be sealed behind a boulder or wrapped in a shroud a moment longer. What wisdom of the church to know the impatience, the longing, that impels us to celebrate now, even while much of the world goes to bed for the night!

Lord, on this Vigil, direct my vigilance toward your reign now and in the fullness of time. Let the words of my waiting for the dawn be gentle but compelling for your peace. Make mine an active longing for the day when your Easter fire shatters the darkness of every human heart, a vigil of joy already, but not yet.

**Today I acknowledge the weeping that still lingers
in the dark corners of our wounded world. I will make
a concrete effort to carry Easter joy to one
still waiting for the morning.**

Reflection:
Longing for dawn

_____

_____

Readings: Genesis: 1:1—2:2, 22:1–18;
Exodus 14:15—15:1; Isaiah 54:5–14, 55:1–11;
Baruch 3:9–15, 32—4:4; Psalm 42; Romans 6:3–11;
Psalm 118; Matthew 28:1–10

Resurrection Grace

*I shall not die, but I shall live, and recount
the deeds of the LORD.*
Psalm 118:17

Jesus surely *did* die; we celebrate not his *resuscitation* but *resurrection.* Yet, herein lies the great joy and wonder of Easter. I, like Jesus, shall die (and probably suffer along the way to my death), but he has burst forth from the darkness of death to open the way for me to a new and glorious life.

Do I fear death, either my own or that of a loved one? How much time, energy, and money do I invest in pursuits that are actually futile attempts to deny or avoid the finitude of my mortal life?

Give me the grace, risen Jesus, to die to those anxieties and distractions that keep me from all the new life you offer me, both for today and for eternity.

**I will celebrate this Easter Sunday by recounting
the resurrection deeds of the Lord to
someone living or dying in fear.**

Reflection:
Dying and rising each day

_____

_____

Readings: Acts 10:34, 37–43; Psalm 118;
Colossians 3:1–4; John 20:1–9

CONTRIBUTORS in order of appearance:

SISTERS:

Anita Constance

Ellen Dauwer

Rosemary Smith

Maureen Mylott

Francis Cordis Bernardo

Kathleen Flanagan

Cheryl France

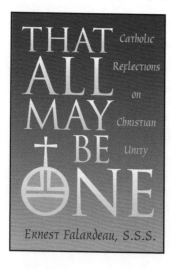

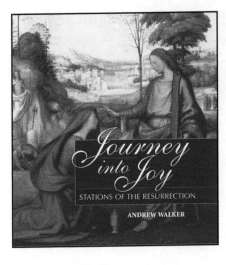

Biblical Meditations for Lent

Carroll Stuhlmueller, C.P.

Readings for each weekday as well as the Sundays of each of the three cycles are summarized, and reflections for each day are given based on scriptural scholarship.

ISBN: 0-8091-2089-5   Price $9.95

*(Price and availability
subject to change)*

Ask at your local bookstore.

*For more information or to get a
free catalog of our publications, contact us at:*

Paulist Press · 997 Macarthur Boulevard · Mahwah, NJ 07430
1-800-218-1903 · Fax: 1-800-836-3161
E-mail: info@paulistpress.com
Visit our website at www.paulistpress.com

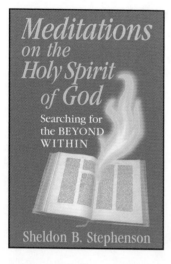

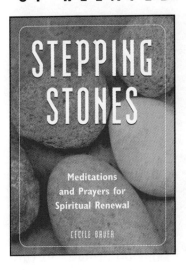

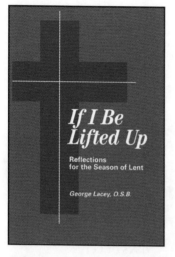

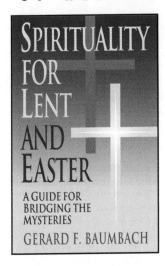

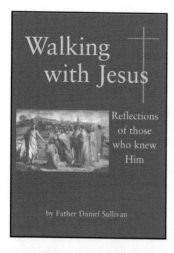

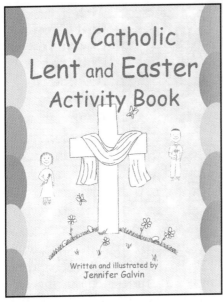

My Catholic Lent and Easter Activity Book

Jennifer Galvin

A book full of fun activities that takes kids on a journey from Ash Wednesday through Pentecost.

Ages 5-9.

ISBN: 0-8091-6706-9 $6.95

(Price and availability subject to change)

Ask at your local bookstore.

***For more information or to get a
free catalog of our publications, contact us at:***

**Paulist Press · 997 Macarthur Boulevard · Mahwah, NJ 07430
1-800-218-1903 · Fax: 1-800-836-3161
E-mail: info@paulistpress.com
Visit our website at www.paulistpress.com**